W9-CBK-394

# Here Is the Tropical Rain Forest

## Madeleine Dunphy

ILLUSTRATED BY

## Michael Rothman

HYPERION PAPERBACKS FOR CHILDREN

NEW YORK

Other books by Madeleine Dunphy:

*Here Is the Arctic Winter*
*Here Is the Southwestern Desert*
*Here Is the Wetland*

First Hyperion Paperback edition 1997

Text ©1994 by Madeleine Dunphy.
Illustrations © 1994 by Michael Rothman.

First published in hardcover in 1994

A hardcover edition of *Here Is the Tropical Rain Forest* is available from
Hyperion Books for Children.

All rights reserved. No part of this book may be reproduced or transmitted in any form or by
any means, electronic or mechanical, including photocopying, recording, or by any information
storage and retrieval system, without written permission from the publisher. For information
address Hyperion Books for Children, 114 Fifth Avenue, New York, New York 10011-5690.

Printed in Singapore.

3 5 7 9 10 8 6 4

Library of Congress Cataloging-in-Publication Data
Dunphy, Madeleine
Here is the tropical rain forest/Madeleine Dunphy; illustrated by Michael Rothman—1st ed.
p.   cm.
Summary: Cumulative text presents the animals and plants of the tropical rain forest
and their relationship with one another and their environment.
ISBN 1-56282-636-0 (trade)—1-56282-637-9 (lib. bdg.)—0-7868-1212-5 (pbk.)
1. Rain forest ecology—Juvenile literature. 2. Rain forest fauna—Juvenile literature.
3. Rain forest plants—Juvenile literature. [1. Rain forest animals. 2. Rain forest plants.
3. Rain forest ecology. 4. Ecology] I. Rothman, Michael, ill. II Title.
QH541.5.R27D85    1994
574.5'2642'0913—dc20    93-24850

The artwork for this book is prepared using watercolor.
The text for this book is set in 14-point Caslon No. 224 Book.

*F*or Claire

—M. D.

Much of the scientific material for this book is based on research by Dr. Scott Mori and Carol Gracie of the New York Botanical Garden. Many thanks for their support, encouragement, and friendship.

—M. R.

$H$ere is the tropical rain forest.

*H*ere is the rain

that drizzles and pours

and may fall every day

in this lush and wet world:

Here is the tropical rain forest.

*H*ere is the frog

who bathes in the rain

that drizzles and pours

and may fall every day

in this lush and wet world:

Here is the tropical rain forest.

*Here is the bromeliad*

that shelters the frog

who bathes in the rain

that drizzles and pours

and may fall every day

in this lush and wet world:

Here is the tropical rain forest.

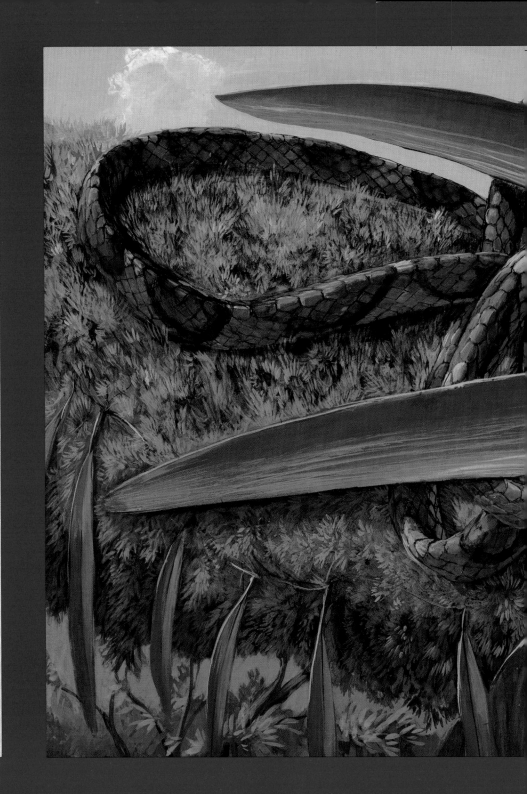

*H*ere is the tree,

which holds the bromeliad

that shelters the frog

who bathes in the rain

that drizzles and pours

and may fall every day

in this lush and wet world:

Here is the tropical rain forest.

*H*ere is the sloth

that hangs from the tree,

which holds the bromeliad

that shelters the frog

who bathes in the rain

that drizzles and pours

and may fall every day

in this lush and wet world:

Here is the tropical rain forest.

*H*ere is the eagle

who hunts the sloth

that hangs from the tree,

which holds the bromeliad

that shelters the frog

who bathes in the rain

that drizzles and pours

and may fall every day

in this lush and wet world:

Here is the tropical rain forest.

*H*ere are the monkeys

that flee from the eagle

who hunts the sloth

that hangs from the tree,

which holds the bromeliad

that shelters the frog

who bathes in the rain

that drizzles and pours

and may fall every day

in this lush and wet world:

Here is the tropical rain forest.

*H*ere are the figs,

which are dropped by the monkeys

that flee from the eagle

who hunts the sloth

that hangs from the tree,

which holds the bromeliad

that shelters the frog

who bathes in the rain

that drizzles and pours

and may fall every day

in this lush and wet world:

Here is the tropical rain forest.

# Here are the peccaries

that eat the figs,

which are dropped by the monkeys

that flee from the eagle

who hunts the sloth

that hangs from the tree,

which holds the bromeliad

that shelters the frog

who bathes in the rain

that drizzles and pours

and may fall every day

in this lush and wet world:

Here is the tropical rain forest.

$H$ere is the jaguar

who stalks the peccaries

that eat the figs,

which are dropped by the monkeys

that flee from the eagle

who hunts the sloth

that hangs from the tree,

which holds the bromeliad

that shelters the frog

who bathes in the rain

that drizzles and pours

and may fall every day

in this lush and wet world:

Here is the tropical rain forest.

*H*ere is the caiman

that fights the jaguar

who stalks the peccaries

that eat the figs,

which are dropped by the monkeys

that flee from the eagle

who hunts the sloth

that hangs from the tree,

which holds the bromeliad

that shelters the frog

who bathes in the rain

that drizzles and pours

and may fall every day

in this lush and wet world:

Here is the tropical rain forest.

*Here is the river,*

which is home to the caiman

that fights the jaguar

who stalks the peccaries

that eat the figs,

which are dropped by the monkeys

that flee from the eagle

who hunts the sloth

that hangs from the tree,

which holds the bromeliad

that shelters the frog

who bathes in the rain

that drizzles and pours

and may fall every day

in this lush and wet world:

Here is the tropical rain forest.

*H*ere is the rain

that fills the river,

which is home to the caiman

that fights the jaguar

who stalks the peccaries

that eat the figs,

which are dropped by the monkeys

that flee from the eagle

who hunts the sloth

that hangs from the tree,

which holds the bromeliad

that shelters the frog

who bathes in the rain

that drizzles and pours

and may fall every day

in this lush and wet world:

Here is the tropical rain forest.

The animals shown below live in the tropical rain forests of Central and South America. Tropical rain forests also exist in Africa and Southeast Asia and in other lands along the equator. Tropical rain forests are very rich in wildlife — half of the world's animal and plant species make their home there.

COMMON CAIMAN

LITTLE HERMIT
HUMMINGBIRD

HARPY EAGLE

THREE-TOED SLOTH

JAGUAR

COLLARED PECCARY

DART ARROW
FROG

RED-RUMPED AGOUTI

TOAD-HEADED TURTLE

BROWN CAPUCHIN
MONKEY

BLUNT-HEADED TREE SNAKE

Like many natural environments, tropical rain forests are threatened by human activities. If you would like to find out ways to help protect tropical rain forests, you can write to the National Audubon Society, RR1, Box 171, Sharon, Connecticut 06069.